For my sons, Jason and Lucas

WHAT IS A TYPHOON, MOMMY?

媽咪，颱風是什麼？

Peter Wilds 著

蔡兆倫 繪

王盟雄 譯

I still remember that terrible day.

"A typhoon is coming," I heard people say.

"What is a typhoon?" I asked my dad.

But he just closed the windows. He looked very sad.

Maybe it will come in the window at night.

Can it do *kung fu? Will it come here and fight?

*為生字，請參照生字表

4

Or is it a ghost with very bad *breath?

Or maybe it's a man wearing black—Mr. Death!

Is it a monster that flies in the sky?

What is it like? Am I going to die?

My brother is bad. He said I am right.

He said I will die in the middle of the night.

He said it has teeth and a mouth like a dog.

And its skin and its legs

are green like a frog.

It has very big eyes

which are yellow like a cat's.

And it has long black wings which are *hairy like a bat's.

I asked my grandpa. Is he right or wrong?

But he can not hear when he's playing *mahjong.

I was not happy. I felt really *scared.

My grandma just told me to help get prepared.

But how can I stop this terrible typhoon?

With a *sword? Or a knife? Or a fork and a spoon?

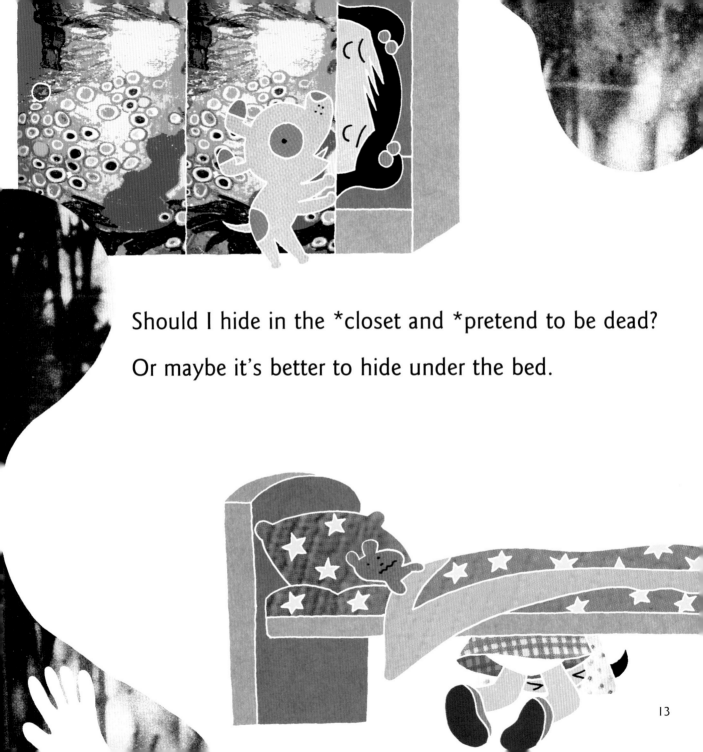

Should I hide in the *closet and *pretend to be dead?

Or maybe it's better to hide under the bed.

13

My mom got some candles, a *flashlight and food.

Why is my brother in such a good *mood?

There's no school tomorrow
because of the typhoon.
"Great!" said my brother.
"We can all watch *cartoons."

We went to the store to buy some more things.

Then we went to McDonald's to eat chicken wings.

I looked at the sky. The clouds were all black.

I said to my mother, "Let's hurry back!"

18

When I got home, I jumped into bed.

"I think I'll be safe if I stay here with Ted."

"Typhoon, typhoon, don't come today.

But you're welcome to come when we are away! "

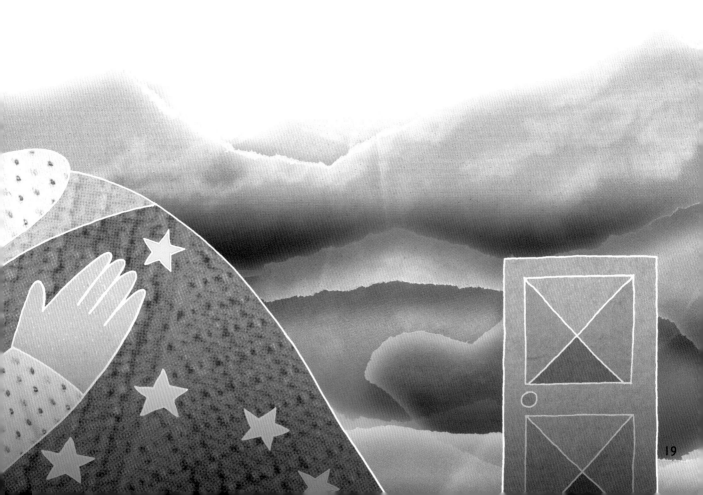

The wind and the rain started fighting outside.

"The monster is coming to get me," I cried.

"Don't be scared," Mommy said. "It will go away soon."

"Go back to sleep now. It's just a typhoon."

"What is a typhoon, Mommy?" I asked.

"Is it a monster that kills people fast?"

"Is it a ghost? Or a man with no head?

Will it come to our house? Is it under my bed?"

"Is it a dragon? Or a snake with ten eyes?
Does it eat little girls? Or just burgers and flies?"

24

"Is it a spider with four hundred feet?
I hope it likes vegetables for dinner, not meat."

25

"Is it a dinosaur, or an *alien from space?

Or is it a *vampire with a *weird, ugly face?"

26

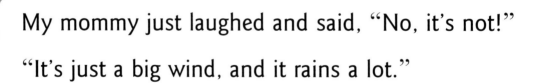My mommy just laughed and said, "No, it's not!"

"It's just a big wind, and it rains a lot."

"It's **not** a big monster?" I said. "It's **not** a big ghost?

It's **not** going to eat me on a piece of toast?"

Mommy just smiled and kissed me on my *cheek.

"A typhoon's just windy and it rains for a week."

"They come in the summer and are gone by the fall.

And sometimes we don't have any typhoons at all."

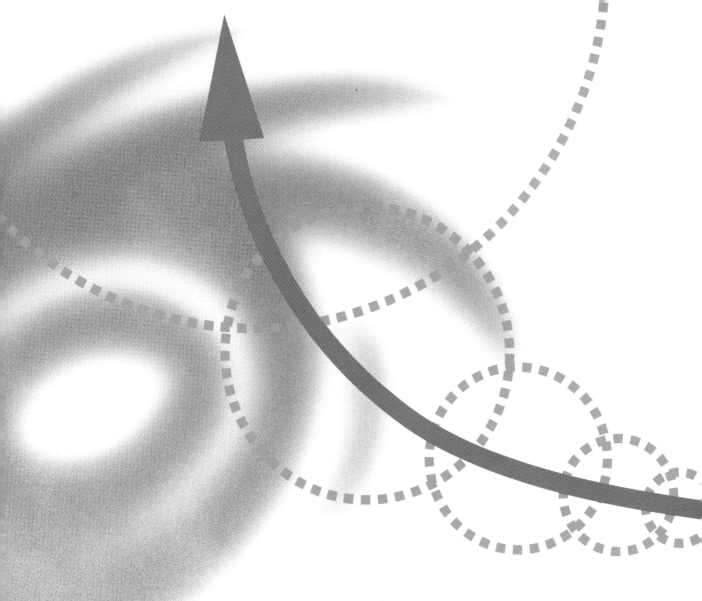

"So sleep now, my *darling. You have had a long day.

There's no school tomorrow, so you can stay home and play."

The rain fell on the window. The wind was so loud.

"Silly typhoon! You don't *scare me. You're just a wet cloud!"

"Oh, thank you, dear Mommy. You're really the best!

Now I know what a typhoon is. I can have a nice rest."

"Good night, Mommy. I'll sleep well tonight."

"*Sleep tight, Jenny," said Mommy as she turned out the light.

"Good night, little Jenny.

Good night, good night, good night..."

生ㄕㄥ 字ㄗˋ 表ㄅㄠˇ

（詞性以縮寫表示：*n.* 名詞，*adj.* 形容詞，*v.* 動詞）

媽咪，颱風是什麼？

p.2 那天真要得，我依然記得，
聽大家說著：「颱風快來了。」

p.3 我問爸爸說：「颱風是什麼？」
他只是關上窗子，一臉難過的樣子。

p.4 或許夜晚拉下黑幕，颱風就會破窗而入，
會不會使出功夫？會不會進來動粗？

p.5 是滿嘴口臭熏天的鬼？
或是死神穿著一身黑？

p. 6　還是妖怪在天飛呀飛？
　　　到底颱風會像誰？可會叫我把命賠？

p. 7　哥哥真是壞，說我很會猜，
　　　午夜一到來，乖乖納命來。

p. 8　他說颱風像惡犬尖牙利嘴，
　　　還有綠色皮膚青蛙腿。

p. 9　像貓咪，一雙眼睛大又黃，
　　　像蝙蝠，毛毛翅膀黑又長。

p. 10　我問爺爺對或錯，哥哥是否在胡說？
　　　但是一上麻將桌，爺爺根本不理我。

p. 11　我可不愉快，差點就嚇壞，
　　　　奶奶叫我來，幫忙做防颱。

p. 12　這颱風真要命，該怎麼叫它停？
　　　　用劍還是用刀砍？用叉還是用匙攔？

p. 13　該躲進櫃子假裝死掉？
　　　　還是躲在床下比較好？

p. 14　媽媽拿來蠟燭、手電筒和食物；
　　　　為何哥哥看起來那麼歡欣鼓舞？

p. 15　因為來了颱風，明天不必上學用功。
　　　　「好，」哥哥輕鬆說道：「大家就看卡通頻道。」

p. 16　我們趕去商店，該買的東西全買遍，
再前往麥當勞，吃雞翅把肚子填飽。

p. 17　我抬頭看看天空，烏雲罩頂黑濛濛，
轉頭便跟媽媽說：「我們趕緊回家躲！」

p. 19　一回家我就往床裡鑽，
有泰迪陪伴感覺心安。
「颱風，颱風，今天千萬別來。
只要我們不在，隨時歡迎你來。」

p. 20　外頭開始風雨大作，我大叫：「怪獸要
來抓我！」
媽媽關懷：「別嚇壞，颱風很快就離開。
現在快回去睡覺，這只是颱風來到。」

p. 22　我問媽媽說：「颱風是什麼？
是不是妖怪，吃人又使壞？」
　「颱風會是鬼嗎？還是人沒腦袋瓜？
會闖進我們家？還是躲在床底下？」

p. 24　「它是隻惡龍？還是蛇有十隻眼睛很兇猛？
它吃不吃小女孩？或是漢堡蒼蠅它才愛？」

p. 25　「它是隻蜘蛛，用四百隻腳走路？
希望它吃素，晚餐沒肉吞進肚。」

p. 26　「它是隻恐龍，或是怪物來自太空？
還是吸血鬼，醜陋怪臉令人生畏？」

p. 27　媽咪笑著講:「別胡思亂想，
　　　　颱風雨很強，狂風呼呼響。」

p. 28　我說:「不是大怪獸？也不是大鬼頭？
　　　　不會將我吐司夾肉，一把送進血盆大口？」

p. 29　媽咪輕吻我，微微笑著說：
　　　　「颱風待得並不久，颱風下雨只一週。」

p. 30　「它們夏天來、秋天走，
　　　　有時連個蹤影也沒有。」

p. 31　「乖乖睡吧，親愛的，今天真夠漫長了。
　　　　明天不用去上課，妳就在家裡玩樂。」

43

p. 32　大雨打在窗戶，狂風陣陣發怒。

「笨颱風，我不會再怕你，你只是一團溼雲而已。」

p. 33　「親愛媽咪，謝謝妳，沒有人比得上妳，颱風哪會了不起，我可以放心休息。」

p. 34　「親愛的媽咪晚安，今晚好好睡一番。」

p. 35　媽媽熄燈並說道：「望妳好好睡個飽。」

「小珍妮，晚安。

晚安，晚安，晚安……」

- 說說唱唱學韻文答案：

p. 47　today, away, day, play

p. 48

typhoon

frog

hat

bed

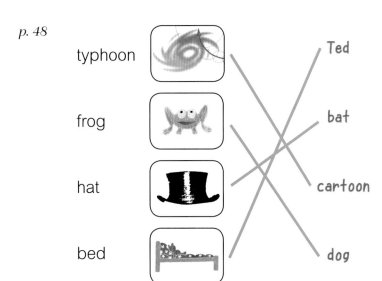

Ted

bat

cartoon

dog

說說唱唱學韻文

唸過前面的韻文之後，有沒有覺得跟其他故事很不一樣呢？韻文跟普通故事的不同，在於多了一份節奏感，唸起來很容易琅琅上口。下面就要告訴你，什麼叫做「韻文」：

請跟著CD的第四首一起大聲唸出下面兩組句子，看看有什麼相似的地方：

a I still remember that terrible day.
"A typhoon is coming," I heard people say.

b "What is a typhoon?" I asked my dad.
But he just closed the windows. He looked very sad.

找到了嗎？答案就在句子的尾端：

a ...that terrible day.
...I heard people say.

b ...I asked my dad.
...He looked very sad.

46

a 組兩個句子的最後一個字 (day, say)，
都是以 "-ay" 的音結束；
b 組兩個句子的最後一個字 (dad, sad)，
則是以 "-ad" 的音結束。

因此，在句尾的地方用相同的韻腳，
就叫做「押韻」。

請跟著 CD 的第五首一起唸，看故事裡有哪些句子，和 "day" 押同一個韻？

"Typhoon, typhoon, don't come today.
But you're welcome to come when we are away!"
"So sleep now, my darling. You have had a long day.
There's no school tomorrow, so you can stay home and play."

（答案請見第 45 頁）

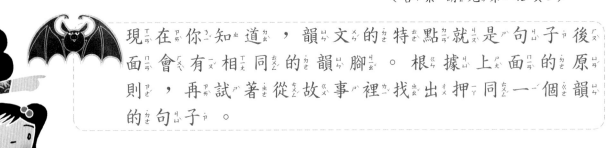

現在你知道，韻文的特點就是句子後面會有相同的韻腳。根據上面的原則，再試著從故事裡找出押同一個韻的句子。

一 CD 的第六首會先唸出左邊四個圖代表的單字，接下來會唸出右邊四個單字；請找出押同一個韻的字，並把他們連起來：

Ted

bat

cartoon

dog

（答案請見第 45 頁）

這裡有一首關於「天氣」的童謠。請跟著 CD 第七首一起唱，再找找看有哪些押韻的字！

Rain, Rain, Go Away

Rain, rain, go away.
Come again some other day.
Little Johnny wants to play,
In the meadow by the hay.

Rain, rain, go away,
Come again another day,
If you don't, I will say,
Rain, rain, go away.

Rain, rain, go away,
Come again some other day,
We want to go outside and play,
Come again some other day.

關於作者

Peter Wilds has authored and co-authored over a dozen books for young people. He has been living in Taiwan since 1993. He currently makes his home in Taichung with his wife and two sons.

Peter Wilds 為青少年寫了很多書，有自己獨立創作的、也有與人合著的。自 1993 年起他就住在台灣了，目前和妻子及兩個兒子住在台中。

關於繪者

蔡兆倫
專長以及興趣：漫畫＋插畫＋圖畫書

關於譯者

貪婪的毛毛蟲，終日啃食忙，爬在一葉葉的文字上，一心只想換上新衣裳。
只要填飽一肚子的好奇，趕快長出翅膀，橫著吃拼音字，還是直著吃方塊字，都不妨。

——王盟雄

童詩、童心與韻文

　　《敲敲節奏說韻文》系列包括三本童書，採用詩歌的形式，為小讀者敘說小女孩珍妮的故事。《我的志願》說的是珍妮的二十五個志願。《越幫越忙》說的是珍妮一片好心幫媽媽做家事。《媽咪，颱風是什麼？》說的是珍妮對颱風的想像。三個故事都以兒童的觀點、兒童的想法來寫，容易引起孩子的會心和共鳴，具有兒童文學的價值和趣味。

　　原作是英文，用淺顯流暢的文字寫童詩。句子都很短，容易學，容易記，背誦不費力。很重視押韻，所以唸起來很好聽。這些優點，使這三本書成為兒童學習英語的理想教材。

　　因為這是一套中英雙語童書，所以三本書都附有中文翻譯，作為呼應，一樣是短短的句子，一樣是重視押韻，既可以幫助兒童了解原

52

文的意思和趣味，又可以避免頻頻翻閱字典的繁瑣而削弱了學習的樂趣。想為兒童選擇英語課外讀物的家長和老師，這三本書值得一試。

兒童文學作家　林良

珍妮是個古靈精怪的小女孩，在「敲敲節奏說韻文」系列中，她以韻文的方式敘述生活中的趣事，有節奏感的故事聽起來好有趣；她教大家什麼是**押韻**，還帶小讀者一起唱**童謠**；她的世界如此豐富，你一定不能錯過！

Children's Verses Series
敲敲節奏說韻文系列

Peter Wilds／著　蔡兆倫／繪　王盟雄／譯
精裝／附中英雙語朗讀CD／全套三本
具基礎英文閱讀能力者（國小4～6年級）適讀

1 What Is a Typhoon, Mommy?　媽咪，颱風是什麼？

2 What I Want to Be　我的志願

3 Jenny Helps Do the Housework　越幫越忙

BUG BUDDIES SERIES 我的昆蟲朋友系列

具基礎英文閱讀能力者（國小4～6年級）適讀

文◆Kriss Erickson　圖◆卡圖工作室

　　我有幾個昆蟲好朋友，各個都有自己奇怪的特性，讓他們有點煩惱；可是這樣的不同，卻帶給他們意想不到的驚奇與結果！

「我的昆蟲朋友」共有五個：

1. Bumpy's Crazy Tail　　邦皮的瘋狂尾巴
2. Fleet's Sticky Feet　　飛麗的黏腳丫
3. Stilt's Stick Problem　史提的大麻煩
4. Macy's Strange Snacks　莓西的怪點心
5. Stinky's Funny Scent　丁奇的怪味道

─附中英雙語CD─

國家圖書館出版品預行編目資料

What Is a Typhoon, Mommy?:媽咪，颱風是什麼? /
Peter Wilds著;蔡兆倫繪;王盟雄譯.－－初版二刷.－
－臺北市：三民，2016
面；　公分.－－(Fun心讀雙語叢書.敲敲節奏說
韻文系列)
ISBN 978–957–14–4677–6　(精裝)

1.英國語言－讀本

523.38　　　　　　　　　　　　　　　95025210

©　What Is a Typhoon, Mommy?
　　　──媽咪，颱風是什麼?

著 作 人　　Peter Wilds
繪　　者　　蔡兆倫
譯　　者　　王盟雄

發 行 人　　劉振強
著作財產權人　三民書局股份有限公司
發 行 所　　三民書局股份有限公司
　　　　　　地址　臺北市復興北路386號
　　　　　　電話　(02)25006600
　　　　　　郵撥帳號　0009998–5
門 市 部　　(復北店)臺北市復興北路386號
　　　　　　(重南店)臺北市重慶南路一段61號

出版日期　　初版一刷　2007年1月
　　　　　　初版二刷　2016年3月
編　　號　　S 806931

行政院新聞局登記證局版臺業字第○二○○號

有著作權‧不准侵害

ISBN　978–957–14–4677–6　(精裝)

http://www.sanmin.com.tw　三民網路書店